Jaguarundi

Otter Cat

by Joyce Markovics

Consultant: Arturo Caso
Research Associate
Caesar Kleberg Wildlife Research Institute
Texas A&M University-Kingsville

BEARPORT
PUBLISHING

New York, New York

Credits

Cover and Title Page, © Animals Animals/Superstock; 4, © Jorge Montejo; 5, © Gerard Lacz Images/SuperStock; 6, © Larry Ditto/Photoshot; 7, © Exactostock/SuperStock; 8, © Arturo Caso; 9, © Arturo Caso; 10T, © Juergen & Christine Sohns/Animals Animals Earth Scenes; 10R, © Animals Animals/SuperStock; 11T, © Rod Williams/Minden Pictures; 11B, © Science and Society/SuperStock; 12, © Rick & Nora Bowers/Alamy; 13, © Michel & Christine Denis-Huot/Biosphoto; 14, © Carol Farneti-Foster/Oxford Scientific/Getty Images; 15L, © CTK/Alamy 15TR, © James Carmichael Jr./NHPA/Photoshot; 15BR, © Animals Animals/SuperStock; 16, © R & M Van Nostrand/FLPA/Minden Pictures; 17, © Gerard Lacz/Minden Pictures; 18, © imago stock&people/Newscom; 19, © imago stock&people/Newscom; 21, © Exactostock/SuperStock; 22, Animals Animals/SuperStock; 23, © Keith Dannemiller/Corbis; 24–25, © Thomas Marent/Ardea.com; 26, © Arturo Caso; 27, © Thomas Marent/Visuals Unlimited, Inc./Getty Images; 28, © Minden Pictures/Superstock; 29, © Arturo Caso.

Publisher: Kenn Goin
Senior Editor: Lisa Wiseman
Creative Director: Spencer Brinker
Design: Dawn Beard
Photo Researcher: We Research Pictures, LLC

Library of Congress Cataloging-in-Publication Data

Markovics, Joyce L.
  Jaguarundi : otter cat / by Joyce Markovics.
     p. cm. — (America's hidden animal treasures)
  Includes bibliographical references and index.
  ISBN 978-1-61772-579-1 (library binding) — ISBN 1-61772-579-X (library binding)
  1. Jaguarundi—Juvenile literature. I. Title.
  QL737.C23M2737 2012
  599.75'5—dc23
                                    2012009600

For more information, write to Bearport Publishing Company, Inc., 45 West 21st Street, Suite 3B, New York, New York 10010. Printed in the United States of America in North Mankato, Minnesota.

10 9 8 7 6 5 4 3 2 1

Contents

A Surprising Sight

In 2008, while jogging along the Rio Grande River in south Texas, Matthew Webster spotted something moving along the ground. "It was a blur at first," said Matthew. As he focused his eyes on the **underbrush**, the sleek, dark outline of a catlike animal became clear. Matthew was certain that he had just caught a glimpse of the **elusive** Gulf Coast jaguarundi.

A jaguarundi is a small wildcat with a thin body, short legs, and a long tail. There are eight types of jaguarundi, one of which is the Gulf Coast jaguarundi.

The last **confirmed** sighting of a Gulf Coast jaguarundi in the United States was more than 25 years ago—back in 1986. When years passed without another sighting, many experts began to believe that jaguarundis no longer lived in the United States. Then, in 2004, several people described seeing the animal at a wildlife **refuge** in south Texas. Those sightings made experts begin to wonder if they had been wrong.

Jaguarundis are slightly larger than house cats. They are shy animals that usually live alone and stay away from people.

In 1986, a Gulf Coast jaguarundi was found on a roadway near San Benito, Texas, where it had been struck and killed by a car. This was the last confirmed sighting of a jaguarundi in the United States.

Hot on the Trail

One of the experts who wanted to find out if jaguarundis were still living in the United States was Linda Laack, a wildlife **biologist**. After the 2004 sightings, Linda was determined to photograph a jaguarundi in the wild. So in December 2004, she hid three cameras in clumps of tall grass in the wildlife refuge where the multiple sightings had taken place. "They're such a mysterious animal that we really don't know a lot about them," said Linda. "That's why we would like to **document** them."

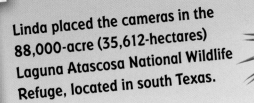

Linda placed the cameras in the 88,000-acre (35,612-hectares) Laguna Atascosa National Wildlife Refuge, located in south Texas.

One of the reasons jaguarundis are hard to study is that their **habitat** is unwelcoming to people. For example, in southern Texas, the areas where jaguarundis may still live are packed with thorny shrubs that people cannot easily walk through. Another reason jaguarundis are hard to study is that they like to stay hidden in their habitat. "They are pretty secretive animals that live in a heavy **brush terrain**," Linda said. "They like to be **camouflaged**."

The color of a jaguarundi's fur helps it blend in with its surroundings—and makes it hard to find.

Biologists believe that a **population** of jaguarundis, related to a group of jaguarundis kept as pets in the 1940s, may exist in Florida. However, there have been no confirmed sightings.

Tracking Jaguarundis

Linda Laack is not the only biologist who is trying to spot jaguarundis. Arturo Caso is also hot on the trail of the wildcats. For more than 20 years, he has been **tracking** these secretive animals in the wild.

Arturo Caso is an expert on jaguarundis and other wildcats, such as this margay.

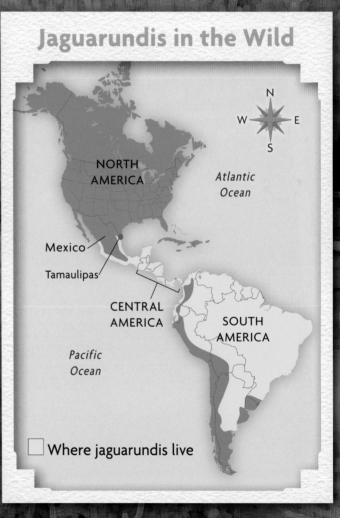

Jaguarundis in the Wild

NORTH AMERICA

Atlantic Ocean

Mexico

Tamaulipas

CENTRAL AMERICA

SOUTH AMERICA

Pacific Ocean

☐ Where jaguarundis live

In the past, jaguarundis have been found in south Texas, Arizona, and New Mexico. Today, scientists don't know for sure if these animals still live in these states. They do know that jaguarundis can be found in Mexico and Central and South America.

Arturo studies jaguarundis in Tamaulipas, Mexico, not far from the Texas border. He has trapped and put **radio collars** on more than 23 jaguarundis. After he has trapped an animal, Arturo weighs, measures, and examines it to see if it is in good health. He then attaches a radio collar, which sends out signals. They allow Arturo to track and study the animal's movements once he sets it free.

This jaguarundi was set free after a radio collar was placed around its neck. Being able to follow wild jaguarundis helps Arturo learn more about how these mysterious cats live.

Jaguarundis are very talkative. They have more than ten different calls that they use to communicate with one another, including bird-like sounds, purrs, screams, growls, and yaps.

Cat, Weasel, or Otter?

Although the jaguarundi is a member of the cat family, it doesn't look like a pet cat. It has a long, sleek body and short, stumpy legs. Its head is small and flat and it has two round ears. Some would say that a jaguarundi looks more like an otter or an oversized weasel than a cat.

A jaguarundi

An otter

Jaguarundis are small animals, only about 21 to 30 inches (53 to 76 cm) long, not including their tails. They weigh between 7 and 15 pounds (3 and 7 kg). Similar to an otter, a jaguarundi has a long, thick tail, which it uses to steady itself when it is running or jumping to catch **prey**.

Like otters, jaguarundis have soft, shiny fur.

German scientists gave the jaguarundi its name in 1803. *Jaguarundi* means "weasel cat" in German. Jaguarundis are also called otter cats, because the shape of their bodies resembles an otter's

Master Hunters

Jaguarundis are masters at finding and catching prey. They use their keen senses of smell and hearing to zero in on animals hidden in the brush. Once their prey is within sight, they will chase it down or **stalk** it. To stalk prey, jaguarundis sneak through the brush, without making a sound. Then, when they're close enough to go in for the kill, they pounce!

Jaguarundis usually hunt during the day, which is when they are most active.

Jaguarundis are also excellent jumpers and can capture prey in midair. One jaguarundi was observed springing almost five feet (1.5 m) off the ground to snatch a flying dove out of the air! With a single deadly bite, the dove became dinner.

A jaguarundi eating a chicken

Jaguarundis like to eat chickens. In some areas, jaguarundis have been known to enter chicken farms to kill and eat the birds. This has made them pests to the farmers in those areas.

What's on the Menu?

Jaguarundis use their expert hunting skills to catch and eat small **mammals**, birds, and reptiles. They won't pass up a chance for fish, either. If a jaguarundi spots a fish in a shallow pool of water, it will use its claws to grab the slippery animal.

A jaguarundi looking for a fish to eat

Most of the time, adult jaguarundis hunt and live alone. Each animal has its own **territory**, which can cover up to 38 square miles (98 sq km).

A jaguarundi will sometimes go after larger prey, too, such as rabbits, opossums, and even armadillos. Although armadillos are covered in a protective, bony **armor**, a jaguarundi can slice through it with its razor-sharp teeth and claws.

Jaguarundis have pointed teeth and sharp claws that can rip flesh.

The word *armadillo* means "little armored one" in Spanish.

A Coat of Many Colors

Whether a jaguarundi is hunting another animal or hiding from one, the color of its **coat** helps it blend into its habitat. If a jaguarundi is well camouflaged, it's better able to sneak up on prey, as well as stay safe from **predators**, such as jaguars and pumas.

Depending on the **subspecies**, the color of the jaguarundi's glossy coat ranges from dark gray to brownish gray to reddish brown, a color similar to that of cinnamon. Scientists believe that jaguarundis with darker coats are more common in the wet, dark-colored forests of Central and South America. Jaguarundis with paler coats are believed to live in drier, grassy areas, such as south Texas, where the color of their fur matches their habitat.

Jaguarundis come in many different colors.

Jaguarundis, like house cats, **groom** their fur with their tongues and paws to keep clean.

A Kitten's Life

Once a year, usually in November or December, male and female jaguarundis leave their separate territories to **mate**. After 70 to 75 days, female jaguarundis give birth to two to four babies, called kittens. The babies are often born inside a hidden place, such as a tree trunk.

When the kittens are first born, they drink their mother's milk for the first few weeks of their lives. At six weeks, the kittens are old enough to eat the same food as adults. After about two years, young jaguarundis are fully **mature** and ready to live alone or start their own families.

A jaguarundi mother taking care of her kitten

Even kittens in the same **litter** may have different-colored coats.

Nowhere to Roam

Before young jaguarundis can start **breeding** and raising their own kittens, males and females need to find each other. This is not as easy as it sounds, since jaguarundis, if they exist at all in the United States, are **scarce**. "I still think there are a few around, but they are scattered and may have a hard time finding each other," said Linda Laack.

Jaguarundis live for about 15 years in the wild and up to 22 years in **captivity**.

Some experts believe the main reason there are so few jaguarundis in the United States is habitat loss. Much of the land they live on is being cleared away for farms, new homes, and shopping centers. For example, south Texas is one of the most rapidly growing areas in the United States. Even if there are jaguarundis still living there, the habitat is shrinking at such a fast rate that it's causing great concern among wildlife experts.

As wilderness areas in south Texas are destroyed for new buildings and homes, jaguarundis are forced to find new places to live.

Critical Habitat

Could there come a time when all jaguarundis are gone from the United States? Unfortunately, the answer is yes. Linda Campbell, an expert on wildlife in Texas, said that unless "**conservation** measures are taken soon, this elusive cat may join the list of species **extirpated** from the United States."

Without help from people, jaguarundis are likely to disappear from the United States forever.

Jaguarundis were first listed as an **endangered species** by the U.S. Fish and Wildlife Service in 1976 and are still considered endangered today. To prevent these animals from dying out, the U.S. government has been trying to help save them. How? Several laws have been passed that prohibit people from killing or injuring these animals. Yet the survival of jaguarundis depends on saving the land they live on. Even though the U.S. government protects jaguarundis from being hunted, very little of their habitat is protected.

To survive, jaguarundis need plenty of land to be able to roam freely and to find enough food to eat.

Fences, such as this one along the border of the United States and Mexico, can make it very difficult for jaguarundis to go back and forth between their habitats in the United States and Mexico.

What Can Be Done?

What can be done to help save jaguarundis? For one thing, the areas where these animals live and hunt for food must be protected from being turned into farms, towns, and cities. Already more than 90 percent of the thorny brush habitat in south Texas has been destroyed.

The good news is that some communities in south Texas are pitching in to help bring the land back to its natural state. They have begun to replant some of the **native** plants jaguarundis need in their habitat. These plants will hopefully encourage jaguarundis to return to areas where they once lived.

Jaguarundis are extremely rare, even in captivity. Only a handful of zoos have them.

Still Hoping

Scientists like Linda Laack and Arturo Caso are still hard at work studying jaguarundis. They realize that the more information people can gather about these amazing animals, the more people can do to protect them from **extinction**.

Arturo working with a jaguarundi

In South America, jaguarundis are sometimes kept as house pets. They are said to be easy to tame and are great at catching rats and other pests. Jaguarundis, however, are best left to live in the wild.

Neither Linda nor Arturo knows whether jaguarundis are still living in the United States. Since she set up the hidden cameras in 2004, Linda has never captured any photos of the animal. This hasn't discouraged her, though. "You just set (the cameras) out, put them in the brush, and hope!" Scientists will continue to remain hopeful as long as people like Matthew Webster continue to spot mysterious catlike animals darting silently through the Texas brush.

Jaguarundi Facts

The jaguarundi's scientific name is *Puma yagouaroundi*. Jaguarundis are small wildcats that have short legs, a thin body, a long tail, and a small flat head. Here are some more facts about them.

Weight	From 7 to 15 pounds (3 to 7 kg)
Length	21 to 30 inches (53 to 76 cm), with an 11- to 24-inch (28- to 61-cm) tail
Food	Mice, rats, rabbits, opossums, armadillos, birds, reptiles, fish, and chickens
Life Span	About 15 years in the wild; up to 22 years in zoos
Predators:	Jaguars and pumas
Habitat	Thick shrubs, heavy brush, and forests
Population	Unknown

People Helping Jaguarundis

Habitat loss is the main threat facing jaguarundis today. At the same time, many people are devoted to saving these animals and preserving their habitat. Here are two organizations that are hard at work helping jaguarundis:

Feline Research Center, Caesar Kleberg Wildlife Research Institute at Texas A&M University-Kingsville

- The Feline Research Center is a wildlife research organization that collects information about wildcats.
- For more than 25 years, the group has used the information it collects to better understand jaguarundis and other wildcats in order to manage and conserve them in south Texas.
- Scientists from the Feline Research Center have educated the public about jaguarundis' home range, habitat, activity, and population.

Defenders of Wildlife

- Defenders of Wildlife was founded in 1947 to save and protect native wildlife in the United States. Today, the organization has more than 400,000 members.
- In 1999, Defenders of Wildlife fought against a building project that would have destroyed jaguarundi habitat and prevented the cats from roaming freely near the Rio Grande River in south Texas.
- The group has also worked to make roadways safer for jaguarundis by providing special wildlife crossings in the United States.

A scientist measures a jaguarundi

Glossary

armor (AR-mur) a protective covering

biologist (bye-OL-uh-jist) a scientist who studies animals or plants

breeding (BREED-ing) producing young

brush terrain (BRUHSH tuh-RAYN) an area of land where small trees and bushes grow

camouflaged (KAM-uh-flahzhd) blended in with one's surroundings because of the colors and markings on one's body

captivity (kap-TIV-uh-*tee*) a place where animals live in which they are cared for by people, and which is not the animals' natural environment

coat (KOHT) the fur or hair on an animal

confirmed (kuhn-FURMD) proven to be true

conservation (*kon*-sur-VAY-shuhn) the protection of wildlife and natural resources

document (DOK-yuh-muhnt) to record information about a topic

elusive (i-LOO-siv) very hard to catch or find

endangered species (en-DAYN-jurd SPEE-sheez) a kind of animal that is in danger of dying out completely

extinction (ek-STINGKT-shuhn) when a type of plant or animal has died out

extirpated (EK-ster-payt-id) completely driven out of a geographic region

groom (GROOM) to clean fur or skin

habitat (HAB-uh-*tat*) a place in nature where an animal normally lives

litter (LIT-ur) a group of animals born to the same mother at the same time

mammals (MAM-uhlz) warm-blooded animals that have a backbone, have hair or fur on their skin, and drink their mothers' milk as babies

mate (MATE) to come together to have young

mature (muh-CHUR) adult or fully grown

native (NAY-tiv) to have always lived in a place; to belong to a place

population (*pop*-yuh-LAY-shuhn) the total number of a kind of animal living in a place

predators (PRED-uh-turz) animals that hunt other animals for food

prey (PRAY) an animal that is hunted by another animal for food

radio collars (RAY-dee-oh KOL-urz) electronic devices placed around animals' necks that send out signals, allowing the animals to be tracked

refuge (REF-yooj) a place that provides shelter or protection

scarce (SKAIRSS) hard to find

stalk (STAWK) to hunt or track an animal in a quiet, secret way

subspecies (suhb-SPEE-sheez) a small category of animals grouped according to similar characteristics

territory (TER-uh-*tor*-ee) an area of land that belongs to and is defended by an animal

tracking (TRAK-ing) following an animal's movements

underbrush (UHN-dur-*bruhsh*) small trees and shrubs covering the ground

Bibliography

The Brownsville Herald
(old.brownsvilleherald.com/ts_comments.php?id=62554_0_10_0_C)

Texas Parks & Wildlife, Publications, Jaguarundi
(www.tpwd.state.tx.us/publications/pwdpubs/media/pwd_bk_w7000_0013_
jaguarundi.pdf)

Read More

Bleiman, Andrew, and Chris Eastland. *Zooborns: Cats!* New York: Simon & Schuster (2011).

Sanderson, James G., and Patrick Watson. *Small Wild Cats: The Animal Answer Guide.* Baltimore: The Johns Hopkins University Press (2011).

Sunquist, Mel, and Fiona Sunquist. *Wild Cats of the World.* Chicago: University of Chicago Press (2002).

Learn More Online

To learn more about jaguarundis, visit
www.bearportpublishing.com/AmericasHiddenAnimalTreasures

Index

About the Author

Joyce Markovics is a writer and editor in New York City. She lives with her husband, Adam, and a spirited rabbit named Pearl, who creeps as quietly as a jaguarundi!